British Columbia

British Columbia

Vivien Bowers

SPLENDOR SINE OCCASU

Lerner Publications Company

LIBRARY OF CONGRESS
CATALOGING-IN-PUBLICATION DATA

Bowers, Vivien.
  British Columbia/Vivien Bowers.
    p. cm. —(Hello Canada)
  Includes index.
  ISBN 0-8225-2755-3 (lib. bdg.)
  1. British Columbia—Juvenile literature. I. Title. II. Series.
F1087.4.W69 1995
971.1—dc20   94-25539
                                                   CIP
                                                    AC

Cover photograph by Jerry Schulman. Background photo by R. Chen/SuperStock.

The glossary on page 72 gives definitions of words shown in **bold type** in the text.

Senior Editor
Gretchen Bratvold
Editor
Lori Coleman
Photo Researcher
Cindy Hartmon
Designer
Steve Foley

Our thanks to April Gill, British Columbian schoolteacher and children's literature specialist, for her help in preparing this book.

Manufactured in the United States of America

1 2 3 4 5 6 – I/JR – 00 99 98 97 96 95

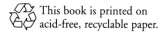 This book is printed on acid-free, recyclable paper.

Contents

Fun Facts

British Columbia is the birthplace of Greenpeace International, one of the largest environmental groups in the world. The organization got its start in 1970, when a small group of people gathered in Vancouver to protest against the testing of nuclear weapons in the Pacific Ocean.

The World Championship Bathtub Race is held in British Columbia every summer. Motorized bathtubs chug and slosh their way across the 37 miles (60 kilometers) of ocean water that lie between the cities of Nanaimo and Vancouver.

Hi! My name is Barkley. As you read British Columbia, I will be helping you make sense of some of the maps and charts that appear in the book.

🍁 The oldest and biggest trees in Canada are found in British Columbia. Some are more than 1,000 years old, growing to over 13 feet (4 meters) in width and up to 300 feet (91 m) in height.

🍁 British Columbia boasts one of the world's largest fleets of ferryboats. More than 40 ferries pick up and drop off passengers at cities along the province's coast.

🍁 More varieties of bats live in British Columbia than in any other province in Canada.

Gigantic trees grow near British Columbia's coast.

The steep slopes of Mount Robson rise 12,972 feet (3,954 m), making the peak the highest in the Canadian Rockies.

Western Wonderland

Imagine that you are in a car heading westward across Canada. Starting near the Atlantic Ocean, you cross the provinces of Nova Scotia, New Brunswick, Québec, and Ontario. You travel in an almost straight line across the flat Prairie Provinces—Manitoba, Saskatchewan, and Alberta. Finally, in the distance, you see a blue wall of mountains. What lies ahead?

Ambling through British Columbia's wilderness on horseback (above), adventurers explore the rugged mountains. *Colorful wildflowers carpet alpine meadows during springtime* (right).

B.C.'s mountains range from striped ridges (left) *to rock columns* (above).

Fasten your seat belt, because you are going for a roller-coaster ride across British Columbia (often called B.C. for short). Canada's westernmost province has many mountains. The jagged Rocky Mountains along the southern part of the British Columbia–Alberta border are just the beginning. As you continue across B.C., you'll ride up and down other rugged mountain ranges. Finally, you'll cross over the Coast Mountains and head down to the Pacific Ocean.

British Columbia covers a vast area. In fact, the province is larger than the African nation of Nigeria. B.C.'s neighbor to the east is the province of Alberta. To the north sprawl the Yukon Territory and the Northwest Territories. A thin strip of the U.S. state of Alaska separates the north-

10

western part of B.C. from the Pacific Ocean. Bordering B.C. to the south are the U.S. states of Washington, Idaho, and Montana.

British Columbia has four main land regions—the Coast Mountains, the Interior Plateau, the Interior Mountains, and the Northeast Lowland. On a map, the first three regions look like a giant sandwich balancing on its edge. The western slice of the sandwich is the Coast Mountains, a narrow band of peaks along the Pacific coast. Mount Fairweather, B.C.'s highest point, soars 15,300 feet (4,663 m) in the northwestern corner of this region.

The Geology of B.C.

B.C.'s mountains began forming about 25 million years ago. Two gigantic plates, or sections of the earth's crust, gradually moved together and crashed. The collision pushed up huge masses of rock. As rock buckled and folded, it piled up into towering mountain ranges.

Then came the ice ages, when thick sheets of ice called **glaciers** covered the land. The glaciers inched across the mountains, scraping out valleys and bulldozing piles of soil and rock. Bit by bit, the glaciers melted away, except on some high mountains. The meltwater flowed swiftly, carving out deep river valleys and filling B.C.'s many lakes.

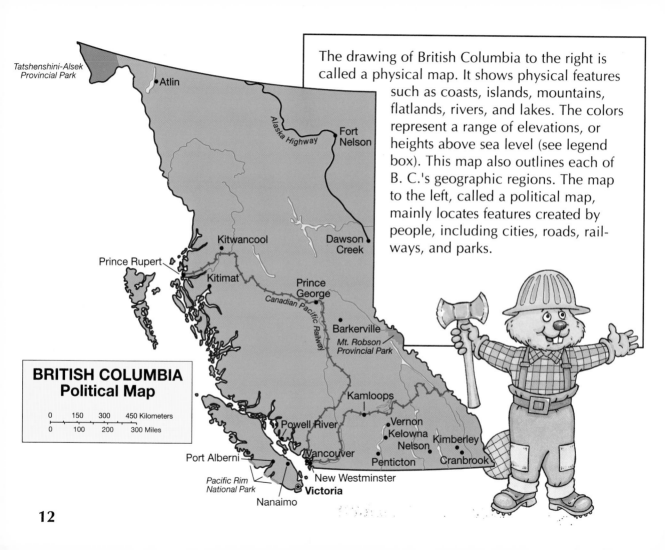

Tatshenshini-Alsek
Provincial Park

• Atlin

Alaska Highway

Fort
Nelson

Kitwancool

Dawson
Creek

Prince Rupert

Kitimat

Prince
George

Canadian Pacific Railway

• Barkerville

Mt. Robson
Provincial Park

Kamloops

Powell River

Vernon
Kelowna
Nelson   Kimberley

Port Alberni

Penticton   Cranbrook

Vancouver

New Westminster

Pacific Rim
National Park

Victoria

Nanaimo

BRITISH COLUMBIA
Political Map

0	150	300	450 Kilometers
0	100	200	300 Miles

The drawing of British Columbia to the right is called a physical map. It shows physical features such as coasts, islands, mountains, flatlands, rivers, and lakes. The colors represent a range of elevations, or heights above sea level (see legend box). This map also outlines each of B. C.'s geographic regions. The map to the left, called a political map, mainly locates features created by people, including cities, roads, railways, and parks.

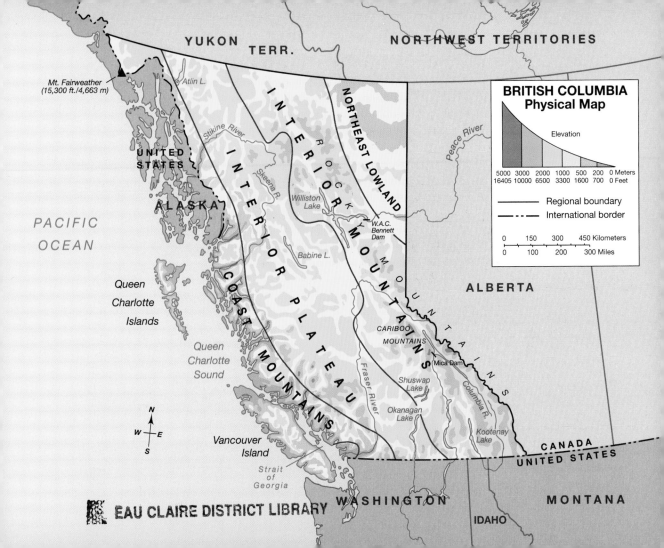

YUKON TERR.

NORTHWEST TERRITORIES

Mt. Fairweather
(15,300 ft./4,663 m)

Atlin L.

INTERIOR MOUNTAINS

NORTHEAST LOWLAND

Peace River

Stikine River

UNITED STATES

Skeena R.

Williston Lake

ALASKA

W.A.C. Bennett Dam

BRITISH COLUMBIA
Physical Map

Elevation

| 5000 | 3000 | 2000 | 1000 | 500 | 200 | 0 Meters |
| 16405 | 10000 | 6500 | 3300 | 1600 | 700 | 0 Feet |

―――――― Regional boundary

―∙―∙―∙― International border

| 0 | 150 | 300 | 450 Kilometers |
| 0 | 100 | 200 | 300 Miles |

PACIFIC OCEAN

Babine L.

INTERIOR PLATEAU

ROCKY MOUNTAINS

ALBERTA

Queen Charlotte Islands

COAST MOUNTAINS

CARIBOO MOUNTAINS

Mica Dam

Queen Charlotte Sound

Fraser River

Shuswap Lake

Columbia R.

N
W E
S

Okanagan Lake

Kootenay Lake

Vancouver Island

CANADA
UNITED STATES

Strait of Georgia

WASHINGTON

MONTANA

IDAHO

At night, millions of shining lights brighten Vancouver (left). *Almost half of B.C.'s residents live in the Vancouver metropolitan area. Vancouver Island— across the Strait of Georgia—has a rocky western coast* (opposite page).

Most British Columbians live in the southwestern corner of the Coast Mountain region. Vancouver—B.C.'s largest city—lies here. To the west of Vancouver, across a waterway called the Strait of Georgia, lies Vancouver Island. From its southeastern tip, Vancouver Island extends 286 miles (460 km) to the northwest. Along with B.C.'s other offshore islands, Vancouver Island is part of the Coast Mountain region.

Vancouver Island varies greatly from one side to the other. Unlike the rough and stormy western part of the island, the eastern section is mild and sunny. The population of the southeastern tip of Vancouver Island is booming, especially around B.C.'s capital, Victoria. Each year more people move to the area to enjoy the mild climate and beautiful coastal scenery.

North of Vancouver Island are the Queen Charlotte Islands. A group of more than 150 islands, the Queen Charlottes are home to many rare plants and animals. Fishing villages and logging camps dot the shores of the islands.

The middle layer of B.C.'s sandwich is a **plateau,** or highland region. Called the Interior Plateau, this upland area contains open forests and rolling grasslands. B.C.'s fruit and vegetable farmers work the land in the southern part of the region. Mining, logging, and cattle ranching are also important industries in the Interior Plateau region.

The eastern slice of the sandwich is another band of mountains. The Interior Mountain region includes the Rocky Mountains. The Rocky Mountain Trench, the longest valley in North America, separates the Rockies from smaller ranges to the west. Logging operations, recreational areas, and a few mines occupy mountainsides throughout the region.

The fourth region, the Northeast Lowland, covers the northeastern corner of the province. Farmers grow wheat and other grain crops on the grassy prairies near the Peace River. Some workers in the Northeast Lowland harvest trees or drill for natural gas.

The ocean and the mountains affect the climate throughout British Columbia. On the coast, the weather is wet and mild. The temperature of the Pacific Ocean doesn't change much, so the water helps keep the air from getting very hot in summer or very cold in winter. In fact, B.C.'s Pacific coast has the warmest winters in all of Canada.

The summer sun ripens crops in the Okanagan River valley (above), *at the southern end of B.C.'s Interior Plateau. The warm, shallow waters off B.C.'s shores are home to anemones* (inset) *and other sea creatures.*

17

Glacier lilies bloom in chilly spots—near icy glaciers.

The Coast Mountains block the warm, wet winds that blow in from the Pacific Ocean. Storm clouds heading inland bump into the mountains and drop their rain on the western slopes, leaving little moisture for the other side. As a result, the interior regions of B.C. are much drier than the coast.

The interior also has colder winters and warmer summers than the coast. Summer temperatures in some inland valleys top 94° F (35° C). In winter the farther north you go, the colder the weather gets. And as you climb up into the mountains, the air grows even colder.

With so many different climates, B.C. has a wide variety of plants and animals. Evergreen forests cover more than half of the province. Western red cedar, western hemlock, and Douglas fir trees thrive in the wettest areas—on the offshore islands and on the coast. Inland, ponderosa pines, lodgepole pines, and western larch trees are common in dry areas. Engelmann's spruce and alpine fir trees grow at high elevations in the mountains. Forested areas throughout B.C. have many different types of plants and shrubs.

B.C. has more types of animals than any other province. Bears, moose, deer, elk, mountain lions, and wolves roam B.C.'s forests. Mountain goats and bighorn sheep climb the rocky mountainsides. Muskrats and beavers live near lakes and rivers, and rattlesnakes slither through the dry grasslands.

B.C.'s coastal waters are home to fish, whales, dolphins, sea lions, seals, and shellfish. One type of fish, the Pacific salmon, spends most of its life in the salty ocean but returns to B.C.'s freshwater rivers to spawn (lay eggs) and die.

A lynx in B.C. (above) **licks her chops after a meal. Off the coast, a gray whale** (left) **dives for food.**

Hundreds of species of birds live in B.C. for at least part of the year. Canadian geese, trumpeter swans, ducks, and shorebirds spend the winter along the mild southern portion of the coast. Other migrating birds rest in B.C.'s wetland areas during their flights north and south.

Fresh water is an important natural resource in British Columbia. The province's many natural lakes include Okanagan, Shuswap, Babine, and Kootenay. Several other big lakes, including B.C.'s largest—Williston Lake—are **reservoirs**. These artificial lakes were created when dams were built across rivers to hold back water. The stored-up water is used to power engines that produce electricity.

Many of British Columbia's rivers start in the Rocky Mountain Trench.

One-quarter of the world's bald eagles nest in B.C.

Sailboats glide across Kootenay Lake in southeastern B.C.

The Fraser River flows south and west from the Rockies and enters the Pacific Ocean at Vancouver. The Columbia River runs south into the United States on its way to the ocean. Another important river, the Skeena, flows into the Pacific about halfway up B.C.'s coastline. Farther north, the Stikine River also drains into the ocean.

In B.C. you can steer rafts down white-water rivers, canoe on lakes, and hike or ski in the mountains. You also can fish for salmon or trout, hunt big game, sail on the ocean, or just go for a drive or a ferry trip and enjoy the spectacular scenery. No wonder the license plates on cars in B.C. read, "Beautiful British Columbia."

Fishers, Hunters, & Traders

No one knows for sure when British Columbia's first people arrived. They probably traveled many thousands of years ago from Asia to North America. Their route went across a strip of land that is now covered by the Bering Sea, off the coast of what is now Alaska. They likely were hunters, stalking caribou, bison, and mammoths. By 10,000 B.C., many different groups of people were settled in what is now British Columbia.

Most native peoples eventually made their homes on the Pacific Coast, on offshore islands, or near major rivers. They made up about 20 different groups, each of which spoke a different language. The largest groups included the Coast Salish, Nootka, Kwakiutl, Bella Coola, Tsimshian, and Haida.

The Raven

The Haida people have passed on stories explaining how they became the inhabitants of the Queen Charlotte Islands. The creator of their world was Raven. In the beginning, Raven put some earth down in the water on both sides of him. One side made up the rugged Queen Charlotte Islands and the other was the mainland. Raven walked along a beach on the islands, bored, until he heard a muffled voice and discovered a large shell nearby. In the shell were tiny beings, who fearfully looked out at him. Eager for playmates, Raven coaxed the strange-looking beings out of the shell. Although they were two-legged creatures like Raven, they had no shiny, black feathers. Instead, the beings had light skin, long dark hair on heads without beaks, and stick-like wings that didn't work for flying. Nonetheless, Raven was happy to greet his new playmates—the first people.

Almost all of B.C.'s earliest inhabitants fished and hunted. People near the coast caught salmon, which they ate fresh and also dried to use in winter. For additional food, women gathered shellfish, berries, and wild plants. Men hunted deer, bears, ducks, sea otters, and other animals.

The coastal groups built huge winter homes, each of which housed several families. In the center of the house, a large, open area surrounded a cooking fire that was shared by all the residents. In summer the people traveled to their fishing grounds and set up temporary shelters.

Woodworkers along the coast hollowed out the trunks of huge cedar trees to make dugout canoes. These artists also carved fancy boxes and fashioned **totems** to decorate the tall poles that they put up outside many homes. Using cedar bark and grasses, craftspeople wove mats, clothing, fishing nets, baskets, and hats.

Coastal peoples hunted sea lions and other sea mammals for food.

Large multifamily homes—such as this Nootka dwelling (above)—gave residents space for social gatherings. Totem poles outside many coastal homes displayed symbols of the clans living inside. Hole-through-the-Ice (right), in the village of Kitwancool, is the world's oldest standing totem pole.

In the dry areas of the interior, food was less plentiful than on the coast. The few groups that lived on the wide plateau between the Rockies and the Coast Mountains settled farther apart than the coastal groups. Inland peoples included the Athapaskans, the Interior Salish, and the Kootenay.

In summer the groups divided into small bands and traveled great distances through the interior to search for food. Along the way, they fished the rivers for salmon and trout and hunted elk, deer, wild goats, and beavers. The Indians also gathered berries and roots. Unlike coastal peoples, inland tribes needed to spend much of their time searching for food, so they had less time for making artistic items.

Most interior groups built their winter homes partly underground for pro-

Tepee

tection against strong, cold winds. In summer they lived in tepees, which could be set up and taken down easily as the people moved from one camp to the next.

Interior peoples traded with both the coastal tribes to the west and the Plains Indians, who lived on the prairies east of the Rocky Mountains. Besides trading goods, the interior peoples exchanged ideas and customs with these surrounding groups.

By the late 1700s, traders from other parts of the world were arriving in what is now British Columbia. Spanish and British sailors visited the coast in the 1770s. They discovered large numbers of sea otters, whose fur was in high demand in Europe. These fur-bearing animals attracted trappers and other explorers to the area.

The North West Company, a fur-trading operation in eastern Canada, sent traders to explore and map the lands west of the Rocky Mountains. Alexander Mackenzie, a trader and explorer working for the North West Company, traveled overland from what is now northern Alberta to the Pacific Ocean in 1793.

Two other traders working for the fur company—Simon Fraser and David Thompson—scouted the Fraser and Columbia Rivers. As they went, the explorers set up new fur-trading posts, which became the first non-Indian settlements in the area. The Native peoples hunted and trapped otters, beavers, and other animals. They exchanged their furs at the trading posts for blankets, iron cookware, guns, and alcohol.

In 1778 Captain James Cook anchored on Vancouver Island, where he met the Nootka people. Cook and his crew repaired their ships and traded European goods to the Nootka in exchange for sea otter pelts.

During much of the early 1800s, another British fur-trading outfit called the Hudson's Bay Company claimed huge sections of western North America. The vast area included what would later become British Columbia, the Northwest Territories, and the states of Washington and Oregon. In 1825 the Hudson's Bay Company built a trading post at Fort Vancouver, near the point where the Columbia River empties into the ocean in what is now Oregon.

In the 1830s and 1840s, U.S. settlers began to move west. The British argued with the Americans over who owned the territory. Finally, in 1846, Britain and the United States agreed to split the land between them. The boundary was set at the 49th parallel of latitude—the same map line that now forms a long section of the U.S.–Canadian bor-

der. Vancouver Island, which dipped south of that line, remained British.

Vancouver Island soon became a British **colony,** meaning it was owned and governed by faraway Britain. In 1849 Britain gave control of the island to the Hudson's Bay Company for 10 years. The Hudson's Bay Company set up their headquarters at Fort Victoria (now Victoria), on the southeastern tip of Vancouver Island. James Douglas, who had run the fur trade for the Hudson's Bay Company, became the governor of the colony in 1851.

The lives of the Indians on Vancouver Island and on the mainland changed as more people came to the area. In general, the fur traders and the Native peoples got along peacefully. But the Native peoples were not used to the alcohol that the newcomers sold them, and it caused health problems among the Indians.

Another problem was that no one knew how to cure the diseases that the Europeans brought with them. Since the Indians had not been exposed to these germs before, many of them died when they caught diseases such as smallpox. The Indians' lifeways continued to change as more newcomers arrived and settled on the land.

James Douglas (above, pointing) *oversees construction of Fort Victoria. As the fort attracted more and more white settlers, Native communities, such as the Haida village of Skidegate* (left), *began to change.*

By the late 1850s, the town of Victoria (above) **had grown into a thriving community. About the same time, gold prospectors** (opposite page) **flocked to the area, lured by the possibility of striking it rich.**

Mines, Pines, & Picket Signs

When prospectors found gold along the Fraser River in 1858, word spread quickly. Thousands of gold seekers heard about the rich finds and came to make their fortunes. Most newcomers traveled up the coast from San Francisco, California—the site of an earlier gold rush. Among these miners were many people who had originally come from China. They were the first Chinese **immigrants** in what is now British Columbia.

Most people came by ship to Victoria before heading to the mainland. Victoria became the supply center for the newcomers. In one day, the town's population rose from 225 to 450 people. A month later, it had shot to 5,000. In all, 25,000 people passed through Victoria in the summer of 1858.

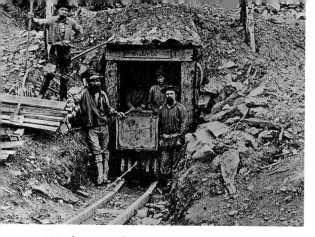

Workers at the Neversweat Company mine pose for a photo.

To maintain law and order in and around the rough mining camps, British officials decided to set up a local government. They formed a new colony on the mainland called British Columbia. The name "Columbia" was taken from the Columbia River, which had been named after the ship of an American fur trader.

Settlements along the Fraser River quickly grew into towns, such as New Westminster, Hope, and Yale. In 1860 miners discovered even more gold in the Cariboo Mountains. The boomtown of Barkerville, in the Cariboo goldfields, soon swelled to 25,000 residents.

Few gold seekers struck it rich. Some didn't even survive. Many miners were unprepared for B.C.'s rugged wilderness. Some drowned crossing from Vancouver Island to the mainland on small, poorly made rafts. Others froze or starved to death trying to wind their way through dense forests and over rugged mountains. Most of the miners left when the gold ran out, and B.C.'s non-Indian population fell to about one-third of what it had been during the peak of the gold rush.

Barkerville, 1865

"Good luck," said Walter, handing his customer the mining pick. "You'll need it," he said to himself as the miner left the store.

"Yet another gold seeker," Walter remarked to Jim, a young store clerk. "One of thousands who have arrived since Billy Barker found gold here in Williams Creek in 1862. Thinks he'll get rich like Billy. Billy made a bundle, of course. Some say his claim made $600,000."

Jim nodded in agreement.

"In only four years," Walter continued, "the town here next to Billy's gold claim has grown to 25,000 people. Barkerville is now the largest city north of San Francisco and west of Chicago! Restaurants, saloons, barbers, bakeries, laundries, a library . . . you name it— Barkerville has it. And don't forget Chinatown where the Chinese miners have their cabins,

restaurants, and meeting hall."

"But most miners here won't make a poke," Walter chuckled. "Sure there's gold in Williams Creek, but it is hard to find. It's down 50 feet (15 m). You have to dig."

Walter stepped out onto the wooden plank sidewalk in front of the store. Like the buildings, the sidewalks were built on log posts above the ground. They provided a good view onto the narrow dirt street. There was always something interesting happening in Barkerville.

"The freight wagon!" called Walter. "I'll bet those oxen are glad to be at the end of their haul. That Cariboo Wagon Road through the Fraser Canyon is hair-raising.

Jim strolled out of the store after Walter. "Still, having a road at last makes things right civilized here in the Gold Capital of British Columbia."

Even though many of them moved away, the gold seekers left behind a very different British Columbia. The colony now had towns with stores, hotels, and saloons. Roads and trails cut through the wilderness. But the populations of British Columbia and Vancouver Island dropped so low that their leaders united the two colonies in 1866. The new, larger colony was referred to as British Columbia.

In 1867 four British colonies to the east—Ontario, Québec, Nova Scotia, and New Brunswick—joined together to form a **Confederation** known as the Dominion of Canada. Politicians and citizens argued about whether B.C. should join Canada. The colony also had other choices. It could remain a British colony, or it could even join the United States.

Nearly three out of four people in British Columbia were Indians. But they were not allowed to vote, so they had no say in the decision about B.C.'s future. Chinese residents and other people of color were not permitted to vote either. In 1871 British Columbia's 12,000 white people decided to join Canada, but on one condition.

In the late 1800s, a narrow road (opposite page) *sliced through the thick forests that once grew where Vancouver now lies. About the same time, work crews* (right) *were building railroads across the province.*

The voters insisted that the Canadian government build a railway to link B.C. with the rest of Canada. The government agreed, and in 1880 the Canadian Pacific Railway Company took on the huge project.

Building the British Columbian section of the railway was not easy. Construction supervisors had a tough time finding laborers willing to work hard, to perform dangerous tasks, and to move frequently from place to place. Between 1881 and 1884, more than 15,000 Chinese workers came to B.C. from China and San Francisco to help build the Canadian Pacific Railway. In 1887 the first passenger train from eastern Canada reached Vancouver.

Many of the Chinese railway workers stayed in B.C. to become farmers, to open businesses, or to find jobs packaging fish or mining coal. Immigrants from other Asian countries also headed to B.C. in search of better-paying jobs. For example, Japanese people first arrived in the 1890s to find jobs on fishing boats. Later, Sikhs—members of a religious group based in India—arrived in B.C. to work as loggers and traders.

Vancouver's Chinatown hummed with activity in the late 1800s.

Not everyone welcomed the Asians. Most Asian immigrants were willing to work for low pay since they could still earn more than they could make in their homelands. Many workers feared the newcomers would take jobs away from white people. And some people disapproved of the unfamiliar clothing and customs of the Asian immigrants.

Canadian officials did their best to keep out new people of color. For example, Canadian laws forced Chinese immigrants to pay a tax to enter the country, so few of them could afford to come to Canada. Another rule allowed only 400 Japanese immigrants to settle in Canada each year.

Native peoples also were treated unfairly. The most important Native ceremony in B.C., the **potlatch,** was banned by the Canadian government in the late 1800s. Officials also forced Indian children to leave their families and go to church-run boarding schools. There the young people learned about Christianity instead of their traditional religion. Often the Indian students were not even allowed to speak their Native languages.

Though illegal, potlatch ceremonies were still common in the late 1800s and early 1900s.

Meanwhile, industries based on B.C.'s natural resources—soil, minerals, trees, and fish—were growing. Farmers began raising more crops as they learned new methods for watering their fields. Along the coast, people packed salmon into tin cans. In the forests, mill workers cut timber and sawed boards. Trains powered by B.C.'s coal carried the province's lumber to the east.

As these resource industries became more important to B.C.'s economy, miners, fishers, and railroad workers began to feel cheated. They believed that they should be paid more money and have safer working conditions. The workers joined together to form **trade unions** with hopes that these large groups could force company owners to make changes.

During the 1910s and 1920s, union workers held protests and strikes, asking for better wages and safer working conditions. Some companies made a few changes. But many businesses simply avoided the strikers' protests and picket signs by hiring replacement workers to get the job done.

Lumberjacks chopping down an enormous tree with axes pause to rest.

His 10-hour shift was over. Tom wearily wiped his forehead with a handkerchief, turning it black with coal dust. Holding the dim flame of his lamp in front of him, Tom trudged toward the elevator that would lift him to the top of the shaft. He was careful not to hold the lamp too high, or the flame could cause an explosion in the deadly coal gas that collected at the top of the tunnel.

Gas explosions had killed hundreds of miners in Vancouver Island's coal mines. Tom knew his kids worried about him every day he went to work. He coughed as he headed down the shaft. With all that coal dust he'd been breathing, he might end up dying from black lung disease anyway. Some life. But he had kids to feed.

"Tom, wait up," called a voice behind him. Tom turned and waited for Harry. "Hear about the meeting tomorrow, Tom? Make sure you come. We workers need to get together and form a trade union. It's the only way! Without a strong union we'll never get the mine owners to improve safety. What do they care if a few of us guys are blasted to smithereens in an explosion? But if we all go on strike and refuse to work, that'll make them do something."

The guys had been talking about a trade union for some time now. But the mine owners were dead set against unions. You joined a union, and the next day you were fired. Then the mine owners brought in workers who would do your job for less money. How could you win against that?

"You'll come, won't you, Tom?" asked Harry.

Tom sighed. "Yeah, I'll be there."

On September 16, 1912, workers at the Canadian Colleries mine went on strike. They wanted better pay, improved safety in the mines, and permission to form unions. By the next spring, workers at coal mines across Vancouver Island—3,500 miners in all—had joined the strike. It was the longest strike in B.C.'s history.

By mid-1914, most coal mines on Vancouver Island were running full-strength with newly hired non-union workers. Unions did not gain a foothold on Vancouver Island for more than 20 years, but by that time, the largest mines on the island had run out of coal and closed down for good.

Tough times continued for B.C.'s workers and businesses during the 1930s. These were difficult years for people around the world. Many Canadians lost their jobs and could not afford to keep their homes.

Vancouver, with its warm climate, became the destination for hundreds of homeless people from across the nation. They hitched free rides on railcars headed west to Vancouver, where they could survive the winters without shelter. Unemployed people marched in protest through the city streets, asking the government to find them jobs or to give them money to survive.

The economy in British Columbia improved when World War II began in 1939. The war created a need for mil-

Thousands of women, such as these loggers, went to work during World War II.

itary supplies, so jobs opened up in many manufacturing plants. Workers in B.C.'s shipyards and mines bustled to produce warships and metals for weapons and ammunition.

Sent Away

World War II brought troubles for Japanese Canadians. The Canadian government worried that these people might be helping the Japanese army, a wartime enemy. It didn't matter that many Japanese Canadians had been born in British Columbia or that some of them had fought with the Canadian army during World War I.

In 1942 the Canadian government sent 20,000 people of Japanese origin living on the B.C. coast to isolated camps in the interior of the province. Forced to move away with little notice, families lost their homes and businesses. In 1949 the prisoners were allowed to return to the Pacific coast. But not until years later did the Canadian government make a special apology and pay for the losses of Japanese Canadians during the war.

After the war ended in 1945, construction companies in B.C. got busy laying new highways and railways. With more transportation routes across the interior of the province, inland logging and mining companies could ship out their products more easily. Other workers in B.C. built huge **hydroelectric dams**. The dams provided businesses with a cheap source of energy for running machines.

A few companies in B.C. began to grow larger in the 1950s and 1960s. They bought out smaller companies

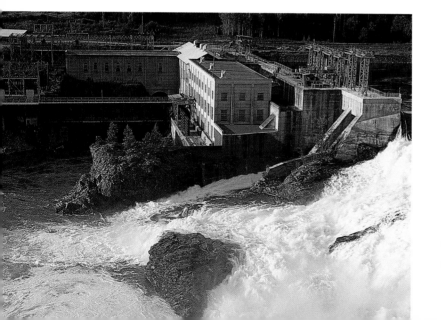

Like other hydropower dams in B.C., the Bonnington Dam on the Kootenay River was built to generate electricity from fast-flowing water.

Whose Land?

When immigrants first began to settle in British Columbia in the 1800s, they built their communities on the lands of the Native peoples. The Indians were gradually moved onto **reserves.** For most of the land they lost, the Indians were never consulted and never received any money.

During the late 1800s, Native leaders began to ask the governments of B.C. and Canada for legal treaties that recognized their claims to the land and that paid them fairly for their losses. For decades their requests went unanswered.

Through the early and mid-1900s, Native peoples in B.C. continued to fight for their rights. Beginning in the 1970s, they held protest rallies, sit-ins, and road blockades. The Indians were not only requesting payment for lost lands but also trying to protect the lands from logging, mining, and other industries. Finally in 1990 the Native peoples succeeded in organizing a task force made up of Native leaders and government officials. As task force members review the claims of each Native group, they hope to reach agreements that will satisfy everyone involved.

and began using modern machines to do the jobs that people had once done by hand. Over time fewer and fewer British Columbians found work in the mines, in the forests, or in the fisheries. As a result, many people moved to B.C.'s cities.

The city of Vancouver has since remained the largest port and the business hub of British Columbia. And with more than one million people in the metropolitan area, Vancouver is also one of Canada's largest cities. Across the Strait of Georgia, Victoria has grown to be B.C.'s second largest city.

Many different groups of people have shaped the history of British Columbia. Some came as hunters, others as traders, miners, fishers, or farmers. And each group has helped form modern British Columbia.

Trees, Rocks, Soil, & Water

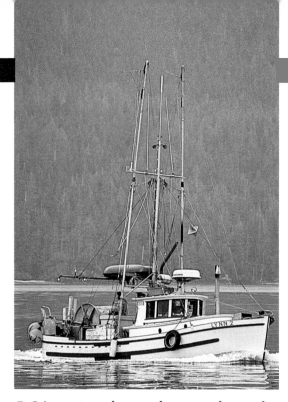

You are flying in a seaplane from British Columbia's capital city, Victoria, to its largest city, Vancouver. It is a short flight over the Strait of Georgia. Below, you see a tugboat pulling a barge filled with logs to a coastal sawmill. A fleet of small fishing boats heads out to the fishing grounds. You can see the coal port, where coal from mines in south-eastern B.C. is taken off trains and loaded onto huge freighters headed for Japan.

B.C.'s ports and coastal waters show a lot about the province's economy. A fishing boat (above) *sets out to sea in the early morning. Freshly cut logs and mounds of sulfur mined in eastern B.C.* (opposite page) *wait to be shipped overseas.*

Your seaplane touches down in Vancouver's harbor, close to the business section of the city. Here people rush down crowded streets past tall office buildings. You've just seen a lot about how people in B.C. make a living.

Just as the early Native peoples relied on the land and water for survival, modern British Columbians also depend on natural resources. Many people work in the resource industries—logging, mining, farming, and fishing. Even more workers have jobs closely related to these industries. These people may sell natural resources or make products from them.

Harbour Centre, one of Vancouver's tallest skyscrapers, features a top-floor restaurant.

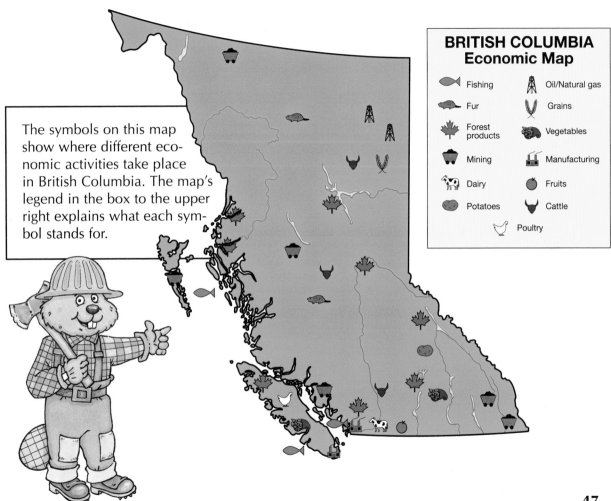

The symbols on this map show where different economic activities take place in British Columbia. The map's legend in the box to the upper right explains what each symbol stands for.

BRITISH COLUMBIA Economic Map

Fishing
Fur
Forest products
Mining
Dairy
Potatoes
Poultry
Oil/Natural gas
Grains
Vegetables
Manufacturing
Fruits
Cattle

The most important resource industry in B.C. is forestry. More than half of the products that British Columbia sells to other countries come from the forest. Lumber for building houses is sold mainly to people in the United States, Japan, and Europe. Buyers in these countries also purchase wood pulp for making newsprint and other paper products.

B.C.'s forestry industry is changing. With new machinery, trees are cut faster by fewer workers. Nowadays only about 23,000 British Columbians have jobs in forestry.

Some people worry that if loggers keep cutting down trees so fast there won't be any forests in the future. Lumber companies have stripped some forests of old growth—big trees that are hundreds of years old. New trees have been planted to replace the old ones, but these younger trees are smaller, so the forests don't contain as much wood. Forestry experts are learning how to best maintain B.C.'s forests to make sure the woodlands continue to thrive.

Soil scientists look for ways to protect the soil from damage done by logging.

Mining is B.C.'s second largest resource industry, although only 1 percent of the province's jobholders work in mines. Coal is the province's most important mineral. Most of the coal is shipped to Japan, where it is used as an ingredient in making steel. Workers in B.C. also mine copper, zinc, gold, silver, and molybdenum (a material used to strengthen other metals). Drilling companies in northeastern B.C. pump oil and natural gas through pipelines to the large cities in southwestern B.C.

Mining companies also have to think about the environment. Government rules control where mining can take place and the amount of pollution mines can produce. For instance, British Columbia's government refused to let one company open a copper mine near two wilderness rivers—the Tatshenshini and the Alsek—in northwestern B.C. People were concerned that chemicals from the mine might drain into the rivers. They also worried that trucks carrying copper from the mine could disturb wildlife. Instead of allowing the mine to open, the government created the huge Tatshenshini-Alsek Wilderness Park to protect the river valleys.

An oil rig in eastern B.C. pumps raw fuel from the ground.

49

Farming is another important resource industry in B.C. About 32,000 British Columbians are farmers. Because B.C. has so many mountains, farmers can use only 4 percent of the land for growing food. But the variety of climates in the province allows them to grow many different types of fruits, vegetables and grains.

Farmers harvest almost all the province's grain in the area around the Peace River in eastern B.C. Dairy cows, vegetables, and berries thrive along the coast where the Fraser River empties into the ocean. By irrigating their crops with water from local lakes, farmers in the Okanagan River valley in southern B.C. can raise fruit trees and grapevines. To the north, beef cattle graze on the grasslands of the Interior Plateau.

The biggest problem farmers in British Columbia face is the spread of cities and towns. Many people want to live in the lower Fraser River valley near Vancouver, where the best farmland in B.C. is located. Farmers there can make a lot of money by selling their land to home builders. But if all the fertile soil is buried under construction projects, British Columbians will lose a valuable food source. The government has put laws in place to prevent building on some of the good farmland.

British Columbia remains a leader among the provinces in the fishing industry. The most valuable catch is Pacific salmon. Other major fish products include herring roe (eggs), fish such as halibut, cod, and sole, and shellfish such as oysters.

Going to Bat for the Fish

Every year thousands of schoolchildren in B.C. raise salmonids (baby salmon) in their classrooms. Starting with eggs or baby fish from a hatchery, the students grow the fish in tanks until they are big enough to release into a salmon stream.

Students at Stoney Creek Community School in Burnaby, B.C., release their fish into Stoney Creek, which flows right by the school. But one day two students, Anita and Alexis, noticed that the water in Stoney Creek was very muddy. They took a water sample.

"When it settled, the jug was about half full of dirt!" said Alexis. This dirt would harm the salmon.

With help from the school's environment committee, the students discovered that the dirt was coming from a house construction project upstream. They contacted the government fisheries department. The government took the house builder to court. He was charged with polluting the stream and was ordered to pay $12,000. Most of that money will be spent to build a new fish ladder so fish can swim farther upstream to reach new spawning areas. People hope the ladder will increase the number of fish hatched in the river.

The students are happy. They say the court case showed people that they can't dump dirt into streams.

"We learned," said Alexis, "that when you've got a problem you should work with a group. It's more powerful."

The students agree that by acting together they got action.

Fishers haul in a large net full of herring.

Many of the fish caught off B.C.'s coast are packaged in local canneries. Packaging fish and other food is an important part of B.C.'s manufacturing industry. In fact, three-fourths of the province's manufactured products come from B.C.'s natural resources. Workers make furniture and window frames from wood and process natural gas for fuel. Factories in B.C. also make some products that don't depend on the province's natural resources. These goods include electronic instruments, communications equipment, and clothing.

Almost three out of four workers in British Columbia have service jobs. Rather than making products, these workers provide services for other people. Restaurant cooks, doctors, teachers, government workers, secretaries, truck drivers, and travel agents have service jobs.

Many service jobs are related to the resource industries. For instance, dockworkers load B.C.'s coal and lumber onto ships, and bankers keep track of the money earned by farmers. Traders sell wood to buyers in other countries, and computer experts help fishery managers with computer programs.

An important and growing service industry in British Columbia is tourism. About 20 million tourists explore B.C. each year, spending billions of dollars on goods and services. Most tourists are British Columbians on vacation in their own province, but many others come from other parts of Canada or from the United States, Japan, Great Britain, and Germany.

These travelers want places to stay, restaurants to eat in, and interesting things to do. Some visitors check in at big tourist centers such as Whistler, a world-class ski resort. But small towns throughout B.C. have also discovered that they can create jobs by attracting tourists to their area. B.C.'s national and provincial parks also draw in many visitors. In fact many people think that British Columbia's natural beauty is its most valuable natural resource.

More than 150,000 jobholders in B.C. work in manufacturing.

A Modern Mixture

A mix of people with different ethnic backgrounds makes B.C. a colorful and lively place. Nowadays most British Columbians have ties to more than one ethnic group. About 42 percent of British Columbians have at least some British roots. People with partly Asian backgrounds make up 19 percent of B.C.'s population. Some residents have ancestors from European countries such as Germany, France, and the Netherlands.

Each year more immigrants arrive in British Columbia. In fact at least one in five people living in the province was born outside British Columbia. Although some people have moved to B.C. from other parts of Canada, many immigrants have come from Hong Kong, China, the Philippines, India, and Taiwan.

British Columbians dance at Greek ethnic festivals (above), *test their skills in log rolling competitions* (left), *and enjoy quiet moments together* (right).

Shoppers at a market in Vancouver's Chinatown select from a variety of fresh vegetables and fruits.

Immigrants have brought their skills, languages, and ways of life to British Columbia. Residents of Vancouver can visit Indian spice shops, Japanese restaurants, and Italian bakeries. Both Vancouver and Victoria have China-towns, where shoppers buy Chinese vegetables, sauces, and noodles.

Immigrants also have brought their traditional festivals to B.C. For example, crowds line the streets to see the Chinese New Year parade in Vancouver.

A Kwagiulth tribal elder beats a drum during a traditional ceremony.

British Columbians also celebrate Oktoberfest, a German festival held each fall.

Many Native groups participate in traditional ceremonies and celebrations. They share their songs, dances, and foods with other British Columbians. Stores and art galleries in B.C. display the work of modern Native artists. Some of these artists are well known throughout the world.

Native peoples make up about 5 percent of British Columbia's population. About one-fourth of the Indians in B.C. live on one of 1,650 reserves. But most Native peoples live in the Vancouver and Victoria areas.

Runners (left) *crowd Vancouver's streets during the annual Sun Run Marathon. In a quieter part of town* (below), *a woman feeds ducks at the Dr. Sun Yat-Sen Classical Chinese Garden.*

A girl gains her balance in a topsy-turvy room at Science World.

In all, British Columbia has over three million people. Two out of three residents live in the southwestern corner of the province, in or near the cities of Vancouver and Victoria. These cities and other places in B.C. feature attractions for everyone to enjoy.

In Vancouver, children and adults alike have fun at Science World. Hands-on displays show how gravity, sound waves, bubbles, and other scientific things work. At the H. R. MacMillan Planetarium, light shows explain what outer space is like. Vancouver's huge Stanley Park has an aquarium and a seaside path for walking, jogging, biking, and roller-blading. Every year, singers, jugglers, and clowns provide entertainment at Vancouver's popular Children's Festival.

Victoria's Empress Hotel, built in 1908, helps give the B.C. capital its old-world charm.

Sports fans watch the Vancouver Canucks play hockey at the Coliseum. The B.C. Lions football team plays home games at B.C. Place, Canada's first covered stadium. The Lions are named after a pair of mountain peaks that tower over the Vancouver landscape.

Both Vancouver and Victoria have long stretches of sandy beaches and calm waters for swimming, sailing, and sailboarding. Skiers and hikers take to the mountains just a half-hour's drive from downtown Vancouver. And since it rarely snows in the city, residents can play golf or tennis year-round.

More than one million British Columbians live north of Vancouver or in the interior of the province. They may not be able to visit museums and big shopping malls often. But they usually have more opportunities than city dwellers to go camping, ride snowmobiles, and see wildlife.

Away from the cities, outdoorsy British Columbians go camping in the woods (left) *and whiz down mountains on snowboards* (above).

61

Totem carvers turn tree trunks into pieces of art at Kitwancool.

Many people in northern B.C. live in one of several communities. Prince Rupert is one of the province's main ports. Many passenger ferries, cargo ships, and commercial fishing boats drop their anchors at the port's docks.

Inland lies the city of Prince George, with the largest population in the north. Many of the community's residents work in sawmills and in pulp mills, where the region's timber is cut into boards or made into paper. Prince George is also home to the University of Northern British Columbia. Dawson Creek, in eastern B.C., boasts "Mile Zero" of the Alaska Highway. This is the starting point of the road that leads from southern Canada to Alaska.

In southern B.C., cities such as Kamloops, Kelowna, Vernon, and Penticton serve as commercial centers for the surrounding region. With so many ski resorts, golf courses, and lakes nearby, people in southern B.C. also play host to thousands of tourists each year. People in towns farther east—including Nelson, Cranbrook, and Trail—are also close to excellent skiing, hiking, and boating areas.

Nelson, B.C.

With its variety of people and places, British Columbia is hard to sum up in one small book. The best way to get to know B.C. is to see it all for yourself.

Famous British Columbians

1 **Bryan Adams** (born 1959) moved as a teenager to Vancouver, where he launched his career as a rock singer. His hit songs include "(Everything I Do) I Do It For You" and "Heaven." Adams's live concerts have established him as a world-renowned performer and as a champion of environmental concerns.

2 **Kim Campbell** (born 1947) became Canada's first prime minister from B.C. and the nation's first female prime minister in 1993. Since her short term as prime minister, Campbell has given lectures and has participated in conferences around the world. Originally from Port Alberni, B.C., the lawyer and politician now has a home in Vancouver.

3 **Emily Carr** (1871-1945), of Victoria, created many paintings of remote Native villages on the Pacific coast and of the area's rugged forests, endless beaches, and vast skies. As a writer, Carr penned the book *Klee Wyck,* which won the Governor General's Award in 1941.

4 **Dawn Coe-Jones** (born 1961) achieved 8 top-10 finishes in the 1993 Ladies Professional Golf Association (LPGA) Tour, becoming the first Canadian woman to earn more than one million dollars in golf prizes. The golfer from Lake Cowichan, B.C., has been on the LPGA Tour for more than 10 years.

5 **James Douglas** (1803-1877) founded Fort Victoria on Vancouver Island in 1843. In 1851 he became the governor of the island. Douglas was named governor of British Columbia in 1858. Governor Douglas, who raised his family in Victoria, is known as the Father of B.C.

6 **Arthur Erickson** (born 1924), an award-winning architect from Vancouver, has designed many famous public buildings in Canada and around the world. B.C.'s government offices and courthouse, Roy Thomson Hall in Toronto, and the Canadian embassy in Washington, D.C., are just a few of Erickson's structures.

7 **Judith Forst** (born 1943), from New Westminster, B.C., is a well-known singer who has performed with many famous opera companies. Forst, a mezzo-soprano, was named Canadian Woman of the Year in 1978.

8 **Seraphin "Joe" Fortes** (?-1922) moved to Vancouver in 1885. Fortes, Vancouver's first lifeguard, made more than 100 rescues, saved 29 lives, and gave thousands of people their first swimming lessons. After Fortes died, a children's drinking fountain was built in his honor at the beach where he worked.

9 **Michael J. Fox** (born 1961), from Vancouver, began acting at the age of 15. His career soared with the popular television show *Family Ties* and the hit movies *Teen Wolf* and *Back to the Future*. Other films starring Fox include *The Secret of My Success* and *The Hard Way*.

Terry Fox (1958-1981) grew up in Port Coquitlam, B.C. In 1977 the young athlete was diagnosed with a rare bone cancer, which required doctors to amputate his right leg. To raise money for cancer research, Fox organized and trained for the Marathon of Hope—a run across Canada. In 1980 Fox began the run, using an artificial leg, but he was forced to quit halfway through when cancer was found in his lungs. Fox's run raised millions of dollars for his cause and inspired the annual Terry Fox Run in Canada. A mountain in B.C. is named for Fox.

11 **Dan George** (1899-1981), or Teswahno, was chief of the Squamish band at Burrard Inlet, B.C. George began acting in 1959. His positive roles in movies such as *Little Big Man* and *Harry and Tonto* helped improve the image of Native peoples in films, which often cast only "bad" Indians.

12 **Rick Hansen** (born 1957), an athlete from Port Alberni, set off in his wheelchair in 1985 to travel 24,901 miles (40,072 km) through 35 countries—which equalled the distance around the world. His 792-day "Man in Motion" tour raised $26 million for spinal cord research and heightened society's awareness of the capabilities of people with disabilities.

11

12

13

14

13 **Harry Jerome** (1940-1982), a world-record holder both in the 100-meter dash and in the 100-yard dash, won an Olympic bronze medal in 1964 and a gold medal in the 1967 Pan-American Games. Jerome grew up in Vancouver.

14 **E. Pauline Johnson** (1861-1913), or Tekahionwake, moved to B.C. in 1909. Many of Johnson's poems, such as "The Song My Paddle Sings" and "Legends of Vancouver," celebrate her Indian and Canadian heritage.

■ **Dorothy Livesay** (born 1909) lives on Galiano Island, B.C. An author and poet, she has written works on a variety of subjects, including political issues and women's rights. *Collected Poems: The Two Seasons* is a book of her poetry.

16 **H. R. MacMillan** (1885-1976) began his lumber career in B.C. in 1907. In 1919 he started the H. R. MacMillan Export Company, which ballooned into one of the world's largest lumber businesses. In 1951 MacMillan became an officer at MacMillan Bloedel Ltd., Canada's largest lumber producer.

16

17 **Nancy Greene Raine** (born 1943), a skier from Rossland, B.C., won a gold medal for the giant slalom and a silver medal for the slalom in the 1968 Olympic Games. The two-time World Cup winner was Canada's Athlete of the Year in 1968 and also has been named the B.C. Female of the Half Century.

18 **Bill Reid** (born 1920) is a Haida artist and spokesperson for Native rights in Canada. The sculptor from Vancouver has carved works in wood, silver, gold, and a rock called argillite. Reid's most famous sculptures include *Raven and the First Humans* and *The Spirit of Haida Gwaii*.

■ **Michael Smith** (born 1932) emigrated in 1966 from England to Vancouver, where he researches and teaches biochemistry at the University of British Columbia. Smith developed a technique to alter human genes. He was named a co-winner of the 1993 Nobel Prize for Chemistry for his discoveries, which are being used to fight cancer and to develop medicines.

20 **David Suzuki** (born 1936) is a scientist, environmentalist, writer, and radio and television host. His CBC television series *The Nature of Things* informs people about scientific topics in an interesting format. Suzuki's has authored an autobiography, *Metamorphosis: Stages in a Life*, and *Looking at Insects/Looking at Plants*, a two-volume set for children.

■ **Ethel Wilson** (1888-1980) wrote novels, short stories, and essays. Most of her works focused on families and friends, and many of the stories were set in B.C. Born in South Africa, Wilson moved to Vancouver at age 10. *Love and Salt Water* and *Hetty Dorval* are two of her best-known works.

Fast Facts

Provincial Symbols

Motto: *Splendor Sine Occasu* (Splendor without diminishment)
Nickname: Pacific Province
Flower: Pacific dogwood
Tree: western red cedar
Bird: Steller's jay
Tartan: blue for the Pacific Ocean, green for the forests, red for the maple leaf, white for the dogwood flower, gold for the British Crown and the setting sun.

Provincial Highlights

Landmarks: Fort Steele Heritage Town, Stanley Park in Vancouver, Butchart Gardens in Victoria, Canadian Museum of Rail Travel in Cranbrook, Hole-through-the-Ice in Kitwancool, Pacific Rim National Park on Vancouver Island, Mount Robson Provincial Park in the Rocky Mountains, Royal British Columbia Museum in Victoria

Annual events: Polar Bear Swim in Victoria (Jan.), TerrifVic Dixieland Jazz Party in Victoria (April), International Dragon Boat Festival in Vancouver (June), Marine Festival and World Championship Bathtub Race in Nanaimo (July), Annual Fish Derby in Kitimat (Sept.), Native Art Show and Sale in Duncan (Nov.)

Professional sports teams: Vancouver Canucks (hockey), B.C. Lions (football), Vancouver Canadians (baseball), Vancouver 86ers (soccer)

Population

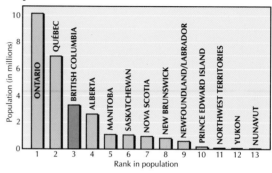

Population*: 3,282,000
Rank in population, nationwide: 3rd
Population distribution: 80 percent urban; 20 percent rural
Population density: 9.6 people per sq mi (3.7 per sq km)
Capital: Victoria (287,900 metro area)
Major cities (and populations*): Vancouver (1,602,500 metro area), Kelowna (75,950), Prince George (69,653), Kamloops (67,057), Nanaimo (60,129)
Major ethnic groups*: Multiple backgrounds, 47 percent; British, 25 percent; Asian, 11 percent; German, 5 percent; Native peoples, French, Dutch, Scandinavian, Ukranian, Italian, 2 percent each

***1991 census**

Endangered Species

Mammals: sea otter, Vancouver Island marmot
Birds: spotted owl, sage thrasher, anatum peregrine
  falcon
Fish: Salish sucker
Plants: southern maidenhair fern

Geographic Highlights

Area (land/water): 365,946 sq mi (947,800 sq km)
Rank in area, nationwide: 5th
Highest point: Mount Fairweather (15,300 ft/4,663 m)
Major rivers: Fraser, Columbia, Okanagan, Peace,
  Stikine, Skeena

Economy
Percentage of Workers Per Job Sector

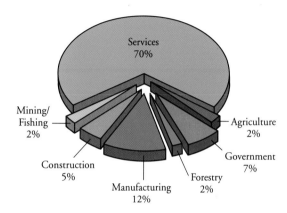

Services
70%

Mining/
Fishing
2%

Agriculture
2%

Construction
5%

Government
7%

Forestry
2%

Manufacturing
12%

Natural resources: forests, copper, gold, zinc, silver,
  sulfur, coal, natural gas, oil, water
Agricultural products: dairy products, beef cattle,
  poultry, eggs, hogs, flowers and nursery products,
  fruits, vegetables, grain crops
Manufactured goods: construction materials, paper,
  newsprint, fish and meat products, fruit and vegetable
  products, metal products, refined fuel products

Energy

Electric power: hydropower (85 percent), fuel-burning
(15 percent)

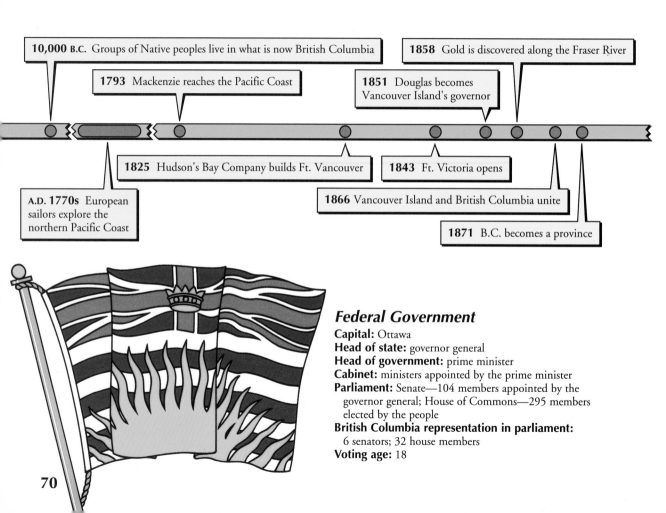

10,000 B.C. Groups of Native peoples live in what is now British Columbia

1858 Gold is discovered along the Fraser River

1793 Mackenzie reaches the Pacific Coast

1851 Douglas becomes Vancouver Island's governor

1825 Hudson's Bay Company builds Ft. Vancouver

1843 Ft. Victoria opens

A.D. 1770s European sailors explore the northern Pacific Coast

1866 Vancouver Island and British Columbia unite

1871 B.C. becomes a province

Federal Government

Capital: Ottawa
Head of state: governor general
Head of government: prime minister
Cabinet: ministers appointed by the prime minister
Parliament: Senate—104 members appointed by the governor general; House of Commons—295 members elected by the people
British Columbia representation in parliament: 6 senators; 32 house members
Voting age: 18

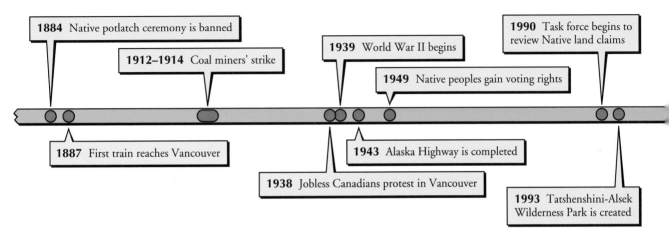

1884 Native potlatch ceremony is banned

1912–1914 Coal miners' strike

1939 World War II begins

1990 Task force begins to review Native land claims

1949 Native peoples gain voting rights

1887 First train reaches Vancouver

1943 Alaska Highway is completed

1938 Jobless Canadians protest in Vancouver

1993 Tatshenshini-Alsek Wilderness Park is created

Provincial Government

Capital: Victoria
Head of state: lieutenant governor
Head of government: premier
Cabinet: ministers appointed by the premier
Legislative Assembly: 69 members elected to terms that can last up to five years
Voting age: 18
Major political parties: Social Credit, New Democratic, Liberal, Progressive Conservative

Government Services

To help pay the people who work for British Columbia's government, British Columbians pay taxes on money they earn and on many of the items they buy. The services run by the provincial government assure British Columbians of a high quality of life. The government pays for medical care, for education, for road building and repairs, and for other facilities such as libraries and parks. In addition, the government has funds to help people who are disabled, elderly, or poor.

Glossary

colony   A territory ruled by a country some distance away.

Confederation   Initially, under the British North America Act of 1867, the union of four British colonies to form the Dominion of Canada. The union gradually expanded as other colonies joined the dominion.

glacier   A large body of ice and snow that moves slowly over land.

hydroelectric dam   An artificial barrier across a river that holds back water for producing electricity. The water is routed to turn huge wheels that power electrical generators.

immigrant   A person who moves into a foreign country and settles there.

plateau   A large, relatively flat area that stands above the surrounding land.

potlatch   A ceremony practiced by Native groups of the Pacific Northwest. The host of a potlatch gives gifts such as blankets, carved boxes, food, and canoes to guests at the ceremony. The more the host gives away, the greater his rank in the community.

reserve   Public land set aside by the government to be used by Native peoples.

reservoir   A place where water is collected and stored for later use.

totem   An animal or other object from nature taken by a family or tribe as its symbol. The images of totems often decorate poles called totem poles.

trade union   An organization for improving and protecting the wages, benefits, and general working conditions of workers who pay membership dues.

Pronunciation Guide

Athapaskan (a-thuh-PAS-kuhn)

Haida (HY-duh)

Kitwancool (kit-wahn-KOOL)

Kootenay (KOOT-ihn-ay)

Kwakiutl (KWAH-kee-yoo-tl)

Nanaimo (neh-NY-moh)

Nootka (NUT*[like put, foot]*-kuh)

Okanagan (oh-kuh-NAG-uhn)

Salish (SAY-lish)

Stikine (stihk-EEN)

Index

About the Author

Vivien Bowers has taught elementary school and has written books, educational materials, and magazine articles for children and adults. Bowers lives with her husband and two young sons in Nelson, British Columbia, and teaches community college courses in writing. She loves to escape into the wilderness for ski-touring, mountaineering, and whitewater canoeing whenever possible.

Acknowledgments

Laura Westlund, pp. 1, 3, 26, 68, 69 (top), 70–71; Peter Langer, Associated Media Group, pp. 2, 44, 55 (center & right), 60; Terry Boles, pp. 6, 12, 47, 69 (bottom); Adrian Dorst, pp. 7, 15, 17, 19 (left), 22–23, 24, 45, 52, 57, 73; Marie Mills/David Cummings, pp. 8, 10 (left & right); David Gluns, pp. 9 (left & right), 11, 14, 18, 21, 42, 48, 55 (left), 61 (right), 63; Mapping Specialists Ltd., pp. 12–13, 47; ©John T. Pennington/Sea-Pen Photographic, p. 17 (inset); George Wuerthner, pp. 19 (right), 49; David Dvorak, Jr., pp. 20, 75; Dept. of Lib. Services, American Museum of Natural History, p. 23 (inset/3844, photo by S.S. Myers); Peabody Museum, Harvard U./photo by Hillel Burger, p. 25 (left); Steve Warble/Mountain Magic, pp. 25 (right), 62; Confederation Life Gallery of Can. Hist., p. 27; Hudson's Bay Company Archives, Provincial Archives of Manitoba, p. 29 (top); Nat'l. Museums of Canada, Ottawa, Canada, p. 29 (bottom); British Columbia Archives and Records Serv., pp. 30 (PDP2898), 33 (HP5191), 64 (upper right/C5229); Vancouver Public Library, pp. 31 (32692), 67 (right) (39374); National Archives of Canada, pp. 32 (C173), 38 (PA45989), 40 (PA116932), 41 (C46350), 64 (center bottom) (PA61930), 66 (lower right) (PA140827); City of Vancouver Archives, pp. 34 (STR.P.276.N.235), 36 (STR.P.351.N.383), 65 (left) (BE.P.115.N.68), p. 66 (far left) (CVA392–602, photo by Eric Lindsay); McCord Museum of Can. History, Notman Photo. Archives, p. 35; Nat'l. Anthropological Archives, Smithsonian Inst. p. 37 (3949); ©Robert Fried, pp. 45 (inset), 46, 56; Ministry of Forests/Forestry Canada, pp. 53, 54, 61 (left); Joseph S. King, p. 58 (left); Lynda Richards, p. 58 (right); SCIENCE WORLD, B.C., p. 59; Hollywood Book & Poster, pp. 64 (upper left), 65, (lower right), 66 (center top); Office of the Right Honourable A. Kim Campbell, p. 64 (center); Jeff Hornback, p. 64 (lower left); Arthur Erickson Architectural Corp., p. 65 (center top); Christian Steiner, p. 65 (upper right); Archives of Ontario, #5898, p. 66 (center); Forrest Andersen Agencies, p. 66 (upper right); B.C. Sports Hall of Fame & Museum, p. 67 (upper left); Fred Phipps/CBC Television, p. 67 (lower left).